CONTEMPORARY LIVES

CEE LO GREEN

RAPPER, SINGER, & RECORD PRODUCER

ABDO
Publishing Company

CONTEMPORARY LIVES

CEE LO GREEN

RAPPER, SINGER, & RECORD PRODUCER

by Stephanie Watson

CREDITS

Published by ABDO Publishing Company, PO Box 398166,
Minneapolis, MN 55439. Copyright © 2013 by Abdo Consulting
Group, Inc. International copyrights reserved in all countries.
No part of this book may be reproduced in any form without
written permission from the publisher. The Essential Library™ is a
trademark and logo of ABDO Publishing Company.

Printed in the United States of America,
North Mankato, Minnesota
092012
012013

Editor: Megan Anderson
Series Designer: Emily Love

Cataloging-in-Publication Data

Watson, Stephanie.
 Cee Lo Green: rapper, singer & record producer / Stephanie Watson.
   p. cm. -- (Contemporary lives)
Includes bibliographical references and index.
ISBN 978-1-61783-619-0
1. Cee Lo Green, 1974- --Juvenile literature. 2. Singers--United
States--Biography--Juvenile literature. 2. Rap musicians--United
States--Biography--Juvenile literature. 1. Title.
782.421649092--dc15
 [B]

                                                    2012945986

TABLE OF CONTENTS

Green's 2011 Grammy performance was colorful— as well as memorable.

CHAPTER 1

A Night with the Muppets

||||||||||||||||||||||||||||||||||||||||||||||||||||||||||||||||||||||||||||||

Cee Lo Green is not known as a performer who does things quietly. When he puts on a show, it's a spectacle.

So when Green was slated to perform at the Grammy Awards on February 13, 2011, the audience knew it was in for something unforgettable. It wasn't disappointed.

Green had been nominated for five Grammy Awards that year: Record of the Year, Song of the Year, Producer of the Year, Non-Classical, Best Short Form Music Video, and Best Urban/Alternative Performance. Green's nominated song had a title so controversial that its name had to be changed to "[Forget] You" before it could be played on the radio.

Also scheduled to perform that night was a singer who was herself no stranger to controversy: Lady Gaga. The year before, Lady Gaga had made headlines by wearing a dress made out of meat to the Music Television (MTV) Video Music Awards (VMAs). Determined to make just as big of a statement at the Grammys, Lady Gaga rolled onto the red carpet in a white egg carried by four pallbearers. Later, during the show, she "hatched" from the egg onstage.

Not to be outdone, when it was Green's turn to perform, he appeared onstage in an enormous, brilliantly colored costume. Huge, birdlike plumage made from red, yellow, and blue feathers sprouted from both of his arms. On his chest Green wore a warrior's metal plate. A bejeweled cap sparkled as he moved his head to the music.

GRAMMY COSTUME

Atlanta-based designer Maria Harper created the costume that had everyone talking after Green's Grammy performance. Harper has worked with the singer for many years and has designed many of his over-the-top outfits. She has created costumes for performers such as singers Jennifer Hudson and Fantasia Barrino and rapper Snoop Dogg.

Harper also designs clothing and interiors.

The costume Harper designed for Green to wear at the Grammys was a jumpsuit that was Velcroed in the front. The wings were worn much like a backpack, and the costume itself was light, but the jeweled headpiece reportedly weighed 12 pounds (5 kg).

Reporting on the Grammys, one writer joked about the costume,

> If [1980s children's puppet television series] Fraggle Rock and the movie 300 had a baby that got hit with nuclear radiation, it would probably look a lot like this.[1]

Green performed the edited version of his nominated hit song, "[Forget] You." If Green's costume and the song he was playing weren't enough to get people talking, his musicians certainly did. Green performed with a band made up entirely of a group of puppet characters known as Muppets, as well as a trio of Muppet backup singers. About halfway through the performance, actress Gwyneth Paltrow emerged onstage to sing along with Green wearing a black jumpsuit, stiletto heels, and pink feathered earrings. Paltrow had helped to make "[Forget] You" famous by singing it during her appearance on the hit television show *Glee*.

The next day the media was buzzing about Green's performance. He'd made headlines not only for the song he'd performed, but also for the way in which he'd performed it. The attention wasn't surprising, considering that Green has been stirring things up since he was a teenager.

MUPPETS INSPIRATION

Green got the inspiration for his Grammy performance from a 1977 episode of *The Muppet Show* he saw when he was a little boy. During the episode, one of Green's favorite singers, Elton John, performed his hit song "Crocodile Rock" wearing a feathered costume and jeweled cap and backed by a musical group of Muppets.

During his career, Green has been credited as a songwriter, producer, and collaborator.

THE CEE LO GREEN SUCCESS STORY

Anyone who watched Green's Grammy performance and thought they were looking at an overnight success would have been mistaken. Green has been in the music business since he was a teenager. It took two decades of hard work and creativity to get him to the Grammy stage.

Green grew up poor in a tough neighborhood in Atlanta, Georgia. He lost both of his parents by the time he was a teenager and had to find his way in the world without their guidance or support. Green could have followed the same path as many young men in his situation, getting involved with drugs and violence and risking jail. But discovering music changed Green's destiny, steering him down a better path and eventually leading him to fame.

> **"As long as you love what you're doing, you should be free to explore."[2]**
>
> —*CEE LO GREEN*

As an African-American artist from an urban area, Green also could have headed straight toward rap or hip-hop music. Green did experiment with these styles. But, always an original, Green decided to do his own thing and created his own unique sound derived from a wide variety of musical styles.

Green has also tried to avoid many of the images commonly associated with rap and hip-hop music. He never cared for the themes of violence, drugs, money, and guns often featured in these genres. In fact, he has criticized some of his peers in the rap and hip-hop industries for the kind of music they make. "It's disheartening to celebrate the guns and the money and the attitude," he said. "You read the words of what these guys are saying and you just say to yourself, 'This is poison.' I don't want to be part of giving that to people."[3]

Instead, Green has given his fans something to think about. He is a performer who never fails to surprise, inspire, and sometimes shock his audience. Green's originality has steered him to the top of the music charts. It has made him not only a hit singer, but also a successful television star, writer, and actor. The little boy who grew up poor

"I am making an only son very proud of me, and my family is proud and supportive. They are living in the moment with me. I am very fortunate to have made a career out of something that I truly love, and I don't have to give off a visage or be a character that I have to play day in and day out."[4]

—CEE LO GREEN

and alone in Atlanta has become one of the biggest and most influential names in the music industry. He's the self-proclaimed "Lady Killer," the "Soul Machine," the one-of-a-kind artist known as Cee Lo Green.

||||||||||||

Green's music draws influences
from a variety of genres.

Cee Lo Green grew up in a rough area of Atlanta, Georgia.

CHAPTER 2

Becoming Cee Lo

Like many other hip-hop artists, Green was not born with the name that made him famous. When he was born in Atlanta, Georgia, on May 30, 1974, his parents named him Thomas DeCarlo Burton.

Growing up in a rough section of Atlanta, Thomas wasn't much different from other children living in the inner city. To survive on the streets, Thomas had to toughen up at an early age.

Both of Thomas's parents were ordained Baptist ministers. His mother, Sheila J. Tyler-Callaway, wanted him to follow in their path, but his true calling was music. He did inherit an almost religious presence from his parents, however. Many years later, that presence would give his performances and concerts a church-like feel.

||||||||||||||||||||||||||||||||||||||||||||||||||||||||||||||

WILD SIDE

Some people might think growing up in a religious family meant Thomas had a strict, conservative childhood. But when he was only two years old, his father died of a heart attack, leaving his mother to raise him alone. From then on, Thomas went by his mother's last name, Callaway. Thomas later said,

I was very young when my father died and it was not something I resented or understood, but I learned to accept there are things in life you can't control.[2]

Although there were always plenty of relatives around—aunts, uncles, and grandparents—growing up without a strong male influence left Thomas vulnerable to negative influences in his neighborhood and at school. When his mother and grandmother tried to reign in his bad behavior, he rebelled.

During the late 1980s, Thomas attended Benjamin E. Mays High School in southwest Atlanta. With his short, stocky frame and creative aspirations, Thomas never quite fit in with the popular crowd at school. An admitted wild child, Thomas had an attitude that quickly got him in trouble. He was the kid the gangs would hire when they wanted some extra muscle. He committed some pretty serious crimes, including torturing homeless people and mugging pedestrians. Thomas said,

I got into an awful lot of trouble. I may have always been artistic but I lacked an outlet, something formal or constructive, so I became . . . destructive.[3]

Eventually, Thomas was kicked out of public school. To try to quell his wild side, Thomas's mother enrolled him at the rigorous Riverside Military Academy. The all-boys college preparatory school is located in Gainesville, Georgia, about an hour north of Atlanta. His classmates were really rough, and one boy in his class was beaten up badly during his time there. Thomas was spared much of the violence because he brought his tough-guy attitude with him from Atlanta.

||||||||||||||||||||||||||||||||||||||||||||||||||||||||||

TRAGEDY STRIKES

Eventually, Thomas learned to see the error in his gangsta ways. He knew the path he was heading down would probably land him in jail. Thomas said,

I could have hurt my mother if I had been sent away for 20 years for some crime I committed. Her life and whole goal of being a success as a

person would have been taken from her and I would have ruined my life, too.[4]

It was music that eventually turned Thomas's life in a more positive direction. But before music could save Thomas, he had to survive another personal tragedy.

> **"Music saved my life. The voice you hear, the soul, the pain, is that of a person who deeply, deeply, deeply appreciates the opportunity they've been given."**[6]
>
> *—CEE LO GREEN*

When Thomas was 16, his mother was in a car crash that left her paralyzed from the neck down. Thomas, along with his grandmother and aunts, had to care for her around the clock. He was forced to grow up quickly, saying,

> *You know, you have to wonder how much living could you have done by 17, but, as we say in the South, I jumped off the porch really, really early. And I don't truly remember the innocence of childhood. I just remember knowing.*[5]

THE START OF A MUSIC CAREER

Thomas's love of music started young. Early on, he was more interested in being a disc jockey (DJ) than a performer. He wanted to be a DJ like Mr. Mixx from the rap group 2 Live Crew and DJ Jazzy Jeff, who started his career in the duo DJ Jazzy Jeff & The Fresh Prince with rapper Will Smith. Thomas enjoyed blending different songs together to create something new and fresh.

Thomas played around with his aunt's boom box, moving the lever back and forth from mono (a single channel of sound) to stereo (multiple channels of sound). As one sound faded out smoothly into the next, it sounded like a

MUSICAL AND STYLE INSPIRATIONS ⅠⅠⅠⅠⅠⅠⅠⅠⅠⅠⅠⅠⅠⅠⅠ

Thomas says his first inspiration was performer Jackie Wilson, a pioneer of 1950s rhythm and blues (R&B) music. He's also been inspired by various 1980s musical acts, including alternative groups such as the Cramps, A Flock of Seagulls, and the Buzzcocks, and rock-and-roll bands such as Mötley Crüe. One of Thomas's style icons was Martin Fry, lead singer of the British band ABC. During the 1980s, Fry often wore a sparkly gold suit. Thomas especially loves Freddie Mercury, the former lead singer of the British band Queen.

cross-fade. Thomas could hear the difference in the sound as the settings changed. His ability to play with music and fuse together different sounds would become central to Thomas's style as a performer later in his career.

Soon, Thomas also discovered his voice had incredible versatility. He could rap full blast one minute, then soar into a perfect falsetto the next. He had the talent—he just needed someone to help him launch his music career.

||||||||||||||||||||||||||||||||||||||||||||||||||||||

BECOMING CEE LO

In 1991, while barely out of his teens, Thomas found a few friends who would change the course of his life. One was rapper Big Gipp, whose real name was Cameron Gipp. When Big Gipp heard Thomas perform for the first time at a friend's home, he knew immediately that he was witnessing a real musical gift. Gipp later said, "I just felt like he was just so fly because it was the first time I had heard anybody rapping and singing."[7]

Thomas, along with longtime friend André Benjamin, or André 3000, and Antwan Patton,

> "[Cee Lo]'s an encyclopedia of music. The things he can reference and talk about in a session are amazing. He spans . . . everything from hip-hop, to electro, to classic rock. We're not in one world. We're constantly blurring the line."[8]
>
> —PRODUCER GRAHAM MARSH

or Big Boi, were among the founding members of the Dungeon Family. This collection of Atlanta hip-hop, soul, and R&B artists eventually produced the groups OutKast and Goodie Mob.

While part of this musical collective, Thomas DeCarlo Callaway was reborn as Cee-Lo Green. He's said "Cee Lo" is an abbreviation of his middle name, Carlo. It's also the name of a game that's played with three six-sided dice. He added Green after he was told he sounded like legendary soul singer Al Green. Over the years, as Green has transformed as a musical artist, his name has continued to evolve. Eventually he removed the hyphen to become Cee Lo Green, the name by which he's known today.

Green got his start in music as a member of the Dungeon Family.

But Green didn't become a household name overnight. It took many years of hard work and creativity, starting with his time with the Dungeon Family and Goodie Mob.

||||||||||

Clockwise from left: Green, Khujo, T-Mo, and Big Gipp formed the group Goodie Mob.

CHAPTER 3

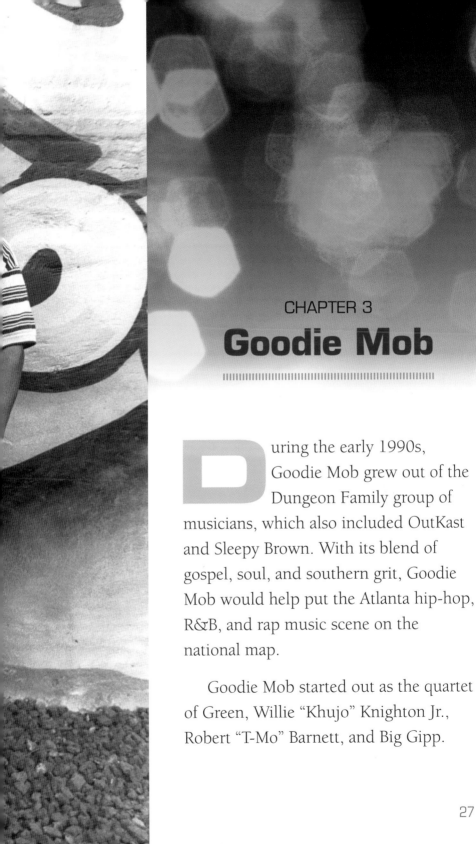

Goodie Mob

During the early 1990s, Goodie Mob grew out of the Dungeon Family group of musicians, which also included OutKast and Sleepy Brown. With its blend of gospel, soul, and southern grit, Goodie Mob would help put the Atlanta hip-hop, R&B, and rap music scene on the national map.

Goodie Mob started out as the quartet of Green, Willie "Khujo" Knighton Jr., Robert "T-Mo" Barnett, and Big Gipp.

The group made its debut on the first OutKast album, *Southernplayalisticadillacmuzik*, which was released in 1994. Green was noticed for rapping the hook on the band's single, "Git Up, Git Out,"

> *You need to get up, get out, and get something /*
> *Don't let the days of your life pass by / You need*
> *to get up, get out, and get something / Don't spend*
> *all your time trying to get high.*[1]

Those early days were lean, and Goodie Mob had to play wherever it could find an audience. The group performed small gigs in clubs and lounges around the South in towns such as Charleston, South Carolina, and Loganville and Macon, Georgia. These towns make up what

THE CHITLIN' CIRCUIT

The Chitlin' Circuit might sound like a tour of southern soul food, but it's actually a name used to describe places where black musicians used to play from the 1930s through the mid-1950s. Before the civil rights movement, very few musical venues were willing to have black musicians perform. The Chitlin' Circuit was a series of small bars and clubs in all-black towns where performers such as B. B. King, Little Richard, and James Brown got their start. Many people believe that by giving these performers a place to play, the Chitlin' Circuit was at least partly responsible for the birth of rock and roll.

> "Everything we do, we do consciously because we feel all music is conscious. I do believe that everyone knows exactly what they are doing [when they create music]. But what they don't understand is the effect of what they say."[2]
>
> —*CEE LO GREEN*

is called the Chitlin' Circuit. The four band members often had to share a single microphone while performing.

Just as Goodie Mob was on the brink of success, tragedy struck again. When Green was only 18, his mother passed away due to the injuries she'd sustained during her accident two years earlier. Green went to his mother's bedside and when he touched her cold hand, he immediately felt an overwhelming transformation. The bad boy disappeared. In his place was a serious musician, devoted to his craft and determined to live up to his mother's dreams for him. Green said of the dramatic change in himself,

> *It's been a miracle, and that's not an exaggeration or overstatement. I have become articulate. I have become eloquent. I have become enthusiastic.*

Goodie Mob spoke to high school students about how music made a positive impact on their lives.

I have become able. It happened all of a sudden, miraculously, when prior to this moment I did not have that aspiration.[3]

Green recalled this transformation years later in the song "She Knows," which he wrote for Gnarls Barkley: "Up, up, and away she goes. . . . And I'm almost sure / I was absolutely nothing before / Now I'm so, so much more."[4]

Goodie Mob proved to be good therapy for Green's grief. "Goodie Mob came along at the right time in my life because I needed that structure, that system, to preserve my sanity," Green said.[5] The other three members of the band became his close friends, and together they shared in Goodie Mob's success. Their 1995 debut album, *Soul Food*, spawned three hit singles. "Cell Therapy," "Dirty South," and the title track, "Soul Food," became regulars on urban radio. Another track, "Free," became known as Goodie Mob's homage to the old-fashioned African-American spiritual. The album went gold, selling more than 500,000 copies.

The group's follow-up album, *Still Standing*, came out in 1998. It had only one hit—"Black Ice," featuring OutKast—but the album still managed to reach Number 2 on the *Billboard* R&B and hip-hop album chart. Similar to *Soul Food*, *Still Standing* features words that go far deeper than typical rap lyrics. Goodie Mob distinguished itself from other hip-hop acts because it had a real presence

In 1958, the Recording Industry Association of America (RIAA) started a program to measure sales of an artist's music recordings. At first, the only certification was gold, which means an album has sold at least 500,000 copies. In 1976, the platinum certification was added. Platinum status is awarded to albums that sell 1 million copies. Multiplatinum status was created in 1984 and is awarded to albums with more than 2 million copies sold. The highest certification is diamond, which was created in 1999 and honors albums or singles with more than 10 million copies in sales.

and a social conscience. "We always felt more like activists than artists," Green said. "We were fighting for the civil rights of Southern hip-hop. That's why we had to be responsible."[7]

||||||||||||||||||||||||||||||||||||||||||||||||||||||||

GOODIE MOB GOES COMMERCIAL

Green and the other three members of Goodie Mob had some success with their first two albums, but fame still eluded them. Meanwhile, they watched their former hip-hop relations, OutKast, rise to the top of the *Billboard* album charts with their 1998 album, *Aquemini*.

In an effort to become more commercial, Goodie Mob signed with Arista Records, the parent company of its label, LaFace Records. The resulting album, *World Party*, came out in 1999. Green left the group abruptly during the middle of the album's production. *World Party* had more of a commercial sound, but lacked the depth of the band's previous two albums. The album was a flop, failing to produce even one hit single.

Arista promptly dropped Goodie Mob, while Green continued pursuing a solo career. The media reported feuds between Green and the other band

AQUEMINI

OutKast was another band to emerge from the Dungeon Family of Atlanta musicians, and they were the first members of the group to find success. Mixing East and West Coast styles, OutKast sealed their reputation as serious hip-hop artists with the album *Aquemini*. The album's biggest track was the song "Rosa Parks"—named for the Civil Rights pioneer, who later sued the band because they used her name without permission. "Rosa Parks" became a hit and earned OutKast a Grammy nomination. *Rolling Stone* magazine named *Aquemini* one of the 100 Best Albums of the Nineties.

Green broke off from Goodie Mob to pursue a solo career.

members after Green left, but he wrote off the bitterness as mere jealousy, saying,

> *Envy was obvious and any jealousy was justified because there was no doubt that I was a jewel. I'd always considered myself an individual in a collective effort.*[8]

Green made it very clear he had been the creative leader of Goodie Mob. "Unofficially, everyone followed my lead because I had the

Bad feelings existed between Green and the rest of Goodie Mob when he left the band in 1999 to pursue a solo career. However, those feelings didn't last very long. "We've never really severed completely," Green told *Rolling Stone*. "We're friends, we're brothers, we're family."[10]

In 2012, Green invited Khujo, T-Mo, and Big Gipp to his hit show *The Voice*. Together, they performed their new single, "Fight to Win." They also joined forces at the 2012 *Billboard* Music Awards to perform a tribute to Adam "MCA" Yauch, a member of the hip-hop group the Beastie Boys who had recently died.

concepts, the theories, and the facts to back it up," he said.[9]

Goodie Mob continued on as a trio, releasing the 2004 album *One Monkey Don't Stop No Show*. It was time, however, for Green to move on solo.

||||||||||||

In 2002, Green released his first solo album.

CHAPTER 4

Cee Lo
Goes Solo

llllllllllllllllllllllllllllllllllllllllllllllllllllllllll

Although music was the most important part of Green's life, it wasn't the only part. In 1997, he met Christina Shanta Johnson at an Atlanta nightclub. She was from Charlotte, North Carolina, and the pair clicked immediately. When they started dating, Green introduced her to some of his favorite things, such as the music of the 1960s rock bands the

Doors and Black Sabbath and the Oscar-nominated Scottish movie *Trainspotting*.

On March 18, 2000, after three years together, Green and Johnson were married. They exchanged vows they had written themselves during a private ceremony at a church in southwest Atlanta. Members of OutKast were there, as well as producers L.A. Reid and Kenny "Babyface" Edmonds, producer-rapper Jermaine Dupri, and boxer Evander Holyfield.

> "Marriage is an old ideal, an institution. It's something that is made out of granite— there's no give. To be married is like being in business with someone. But marriage will make you a man."[2]
>
> —CEE LO GREEN

Green had issued a statement announcing his impending nuptials. "This marriage is a fulfillment of prophecy, so in that sense I feel a calm and an assurance . . . about my love and my choice in a woman and a soul mate," he wrote.[1] He called Johnson "the other half of my whole," and said she had "filled a void in me personally, spiritually, mentally, professionally, and emotionally."[3]

The couple settled in Fayetteville, a suburb just south of Atlanta. Johnson already had two daughters—Sierra and Kalah. Though he was still only in his twenties, Green became a doting father, adopting the two girls.

Soon, Green and Johnson had their own child. In 2000, their son, Kingston, was born. "Everyone speaks highly of their kids, but I've got a very smart little boy!" Green said in one interview.

GRANDPA CEE LO

In 2010, Green became a grandfather at age 35 when Sierra had a baby boy. Becoming a grandfather at a young age didn't bother Green in the least. "How I overcome it is by just thinking of myself as the coolest, hippest, freshest granddad you ever met," he said.[4] When she was 15, Sierra had been featured in an episode of the first season of the MTV series *My Super Sweet 16*. Sierra was shown arriving at her super-charged birthday party via helicopter. Today, Sierra is a singer like her famous father and has also released a line of makeup. Sierra has called her dad one of her greatest inspirations, saying, "I know I'm very lucky. I have an awesome dad who is also a great role model."[5]

Green with his family in 2011

"He's not overwhelmed by me being a celebrity. He gets the dad side of me."[6]

SOLO ACT

Musically, Green spread his creative wings on his 2002 solo debut for Arista Records, *Cee-Lo and His Perfect Imperfections*. Finally able to express himself without a band to hold him back, Green steered away from his hip-hop and rap roots. The 21 songs on the album were a lesson in musical diversity, combining sounds adopted from genres such as hip-hop, soul, rock, funk, pop, and gospel.

For Green, having total control over his own music was a welcome departure. "I've always kept in mind what I wanted to do as an individual. I'm broad in influence and rich in possibility," Green said. "So, for lack of a medium and being engulfed in what Goodie Mob was doing, I was unable to do that. I felt now was the time to express myself. . . ."[7]

Ben Allen, Green's recording engineer, said this "new" sound wasn't really new at all for Green:

> The people that Cee Lo knows in the music business have seen him as this urban artist for so long. He's really not an urban artist. I think

BREAKING THE MOLD |||||||||||||||||||||||||||||||||||||||||||||||||||||||||||||||||||

For his album *Cee-Lo and His Perfect Imperfections*, Green wrote the song "Closet Freak" about his barber, Menta. It turned out the tune was really about him being an innovative artist in a conformist music industry. Green said,

"I wrote the song for him. But it ended up being about me and how I see myself coming out with this creative vocal act of individualism in the midst of marketplace monotony."[8]

he's an international, avant-garde, experimental artist.[9]

The album struck a chord with both record executives and critics. "Everything Cee Lo is doing is original," said Arista executive vice president Lionel Ridenour. "He's giving a whole new meaning to creative expression from a hip-hop foundation."[10] *Entertainment Weekly* reviewer Will Hermes said Green "explodes like a man released from creative prison."[11] *Cee Lo and His Perfect Imperfections* earned Green a 2003 Grammy

"CLOSET FREAK"

Green has become known for his flamboyant style. In the video for "Closet Freak," Green expresses his inner freak by strutting around in a white feather boa, a black cape with wings, a preacher's robe, and a wig. Green bought an orange wig, a kimono, and clogs at a Los Angeles boutique, which he wore to a performance at an Atlanta concert hall. Cedric "Ced Keys" Williams, a musician touring with Green, said, "He walks out, and folks just went crazy, man."[12] Green was also photographed on another occasion wearing a white lace wedding grown.

Green has extended his stylistic creativity to his own skin. His face, head, and body are covered in a layer of tattoos. At one time he even considered getting his entire face tattooed. Green has one unfinished tattoo on his back, a family tree, which he has said he found too painful to complete.

nomination for the single "Gettin' Grown," an upbeat song with a light but infectious beat.

||||||||||||||||||||||||||||||||||||||||||||||||||||||||||||||

CEE LO GREEN . . . IS THE SOUL MACHINE

In 2004 came another solo effort, *Cee-Lo Green . . . Is the Soul Machine*. It features some of the biggest hip-hop musicians of the time, including Timbaland, Pharrell, and Ludacris. On this and his other albums, Green distinguishes himself from other artists of his generation by using real instruments—not just artificial synthesizers and drum machines. His albums feature a blend of horns, guitars, and complex vocal harmonies. Green said,

> *Sometimes it seems as if, if music isn't produced with live instrumentation, or some element of live instrumentation, then it is not alive. The synthetic does not have a soul.*[13]

Green has also chosen to delve deeper than some of his fellow musicians when writing songs. He covers subjects that have much greater importance than flashy cars, money, and the other

Cee-Lo Green . . . Is the Soul Machine debuted at Number 2 on the Billboard R&B/Hip-Hop album chart.

shallow pursuits favored by many hip-hop acts. Green has said:

> *In these bleak days and times, I feel like I'm morally obligated to be expressive, and I have a vehicle to speak from, to make relevant the issues and topics of today.*[14]

The goal of Green's music, he says, is to "encourage others to think, to consider, and to question."[15] On *Cee-Lo Green...Is the Soul Machine*, he sings about his disdain for other hip-hop artists, particularly in the song "Scrap Metal."

Journalists who reviewed Green's solo efforts were quick to recognize his unique abilities, comparing him to other soul and funk pioneers, including artists Prince and De La Soul. One reviewer called his second album "one of the most ambitious albums to come out of any genre in recent times."[16]

||||||||||

Green's producer, Jazze Pha, *left*, has collaborated with hip-hop artists such as Lil Wayne and Ludacris.

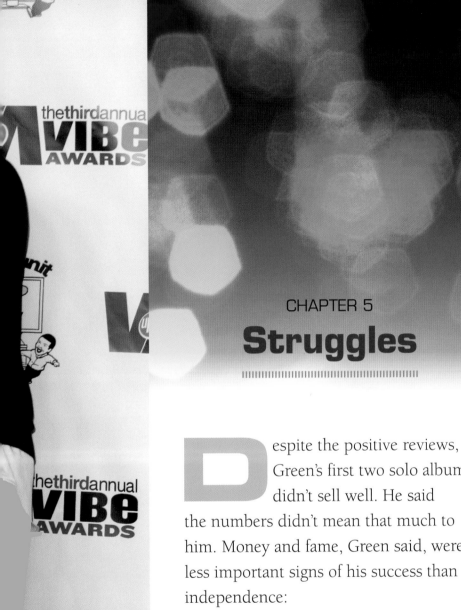

thethirdannua
VIBe
AWARDS

nit

thethirdannual
VIBe
AWARDS

OR

thethirdannual
VIBe
AWARDS

CHAPTER 5

Struggles

||||||||||||||||||||||||||||||||||||||||||||||||||||||||||||

Despite the positive reviews, Green's first two solo albums didn't sell well. He said the numbers didn't mean that much to him. Money and fame, Green said, were less important signs of his success than independence:

My early solo albums were not huge sellers, but I remained true to myself. I had to take charge and remained obedient to my own instinct and impulses. I was sure I was moving forward and my work was not in vain. No one was going to stop me from doing my own thing.[1]

In 2005, parent company Sony BMG restructured Green's longtime label, Arista Records. Rather than get lost in the shuffle, Green asked to be released from his contract and became a free agent. Instead of lamenting the loss of his record deal, Green took advantage of the time on his own to continue expressing himself creatively. Since he didn't have a contract, it was also easier for him to move around.

Green was still able to record music, but now it was on his own terms. He decided to start forming his own label, Radiculture Records, in Atlanta,

RADICULTURE RECORDS |||||||||||||||||||||||||||||||||||||||||||||||||||||||||||||||||||

Green formed Atlanta-based Radiculture Records with his manager KC Morton in 2004, around the same time that his second solo album, *Cee-Lo Green . . . Is the Soul Machine*, was released. The label began nurturing new artists, including Tori Alamaze and the hip-hop and soul act Kirkland Underwater. However, official launch of the label was put on hold until 2007. The label prides itself on working with acts too alternative for the mainstream music industry. Its motto is: "We don't compete or compare, we coexist."[2]

||||||||||||||||||||||||||||||||||||||||||||||||||||||||||||||||||||||||||||||||||||||||||

While Green isn't typically associated with pop girl group the Pussycat Dolls, he was actually responsible for their very first hit. Green originally wrote and produced the song in 2004 for an Atlanta-based performer named Tori Alamaze. Alamaze had been a backup singer for OutKast and was signed to Universal Records as a solo artist. Her version of the song only reached Number 53 on *Billboard's* R&B/Hip-Hop Chart. Universal dropped Alamaze before the release of her album and asked Green to rerecord the song for the Pussycat Dolls. The Pussycat Dolls' version, however, climbed to Number 2 on the *Billboard* Hot 100. "Don't Cha" eventually went platinum and had sold more than 2 million downloads as of January 2010. Today, few people realize Green was originally behind the hit.

Georgia. He also mentored a new generation of artists, including local singer Tori Alamaze and Kirkland Underwater. Green collaborated with acts such as OutKast, Kelis, Jack Splash, and the Black Eyed Peas. And he released an album called *Happy Hour* with Sho 'Nuff Records producer Jazze Pha.

||||||||||||||||||||||||||||||||||||||||||||||||||||||||

MARRIAGE TROUBLE

By all accounts, Johnson and Green started out
with a solid, loving marriage. In fact, Johnson once
described her husband as "a really good man with a
sweet heart."[3] Yet there had been problems growing
in their relationship.

Green was upset over the stagnant progress
of his solo career and embroiled in battles with
his record company—stresses that were spilling
over into his marriage. "It was very emotional
and upsetting," Johnson later said. "That's when
everything started getting turbulent. . . . It wasn't a
happy time."[4]

In one early incident, Johnson called the police
after Green threw a wooden statue through the
window of the couple's car in July 2001. Green
was arrested on charges of assault and disorderly
conduct. When he didn't show up at his September
court date, he was arrested again and spent two
days in jail. Eventually, Green was put on probation
for one year. During this time, he was required to
attend domestic violence counseling and submit to
random drug and alcohol tests.

||||||||||||||||||||||||||||||||||||||||||||||||||||||||

DIVORCE

The couple tried to make its marriage work,
but it didn't last. In May 2004, Johnson filed for
divorce. They finalized the divorce in August 2005.
Although the court awarded the couple joint legal
custody of their son, Kingston was sent to live
permanently with his mother.

Despite their divorce, the former couple does
not hold bitter feelings for one another. Johnson
seemed to understand the difficulties of Green's
career. "I think you can't be going through
something outside and then come inside the house
and it's gone," Johnson said. "I think if you're going
through things emotionally, it's going to affect every
other aspect of your life."[5]

LEGACY CAR

After Green's mother passed away, he gave himself a present with the insurance money he inherited—a 1965 Chevy Impala Super Sport. "It's a beautiful sea-foam green color, like a teal green, white interior—it's just a gorgeous car," Green said.[6] The Impala was one of the first cars he bought for himself during his Goodie Mob days, and he has big plans for it. "I haven't driven it in years, so it's just parked and being preserved. I really want my son to have it years from now," he said.[7]

Green doesn't have the kind of looks that would typically make women swoon. He's short, squat, and bald. *Rolling Stone* magazine once described him as "roughly as tall as a mini-refrigerator and as broad as a Hummer."[9] But according to Green, he's never had trouble getting women—including former wife Johnson. He even refers to himself on an album and on his Web site as "the Lady Killer." Green may not be classically handsome, but he's definitely cool. "I've been such an oddball my whole life, but I've always been cool and I've always dressed fairly smartly," he said.[10]

And Green continued to have feelings for his ex-wife long after he signed the divorce papers. Johnson, Sierra, Kalah, and Kingston have even appeared with Green during red carpet events. "Christina has my heart," he said. "That's my sister. I love her like that. She's a strong girl. She stuck with me through a rough time. And we had some good times, too."[8]

Still, Green was looking forward to being single—especially since his career was getting back on track and he was making a name for himself in the music business. Green's name started becoming even more recognizable as he developed

Green mentored other artists even as he experienced a period of
personal and professional struggles.

a partnership with a producer named Danger
Mouse. Their collaboration would help ignite
Green's career.

||||||||||

Danger Mouse, *left*, impressed
Green with his musical mash-ups.

CHAPTER 6

Gnarls Barkley

‖‖‖

I n 1998, Green received a demo tape from a young hip-hop musician named Brian Burton. Like Green, Burton had been raised on musical diversity, listening to everything from 1960s psychedelic rock to 1980s hair metal to 1990s hip-hop while growing up in New York.

Burton later started going by the name Danger Mouse, from the 1980s British cartoon series. But he continued to be a big fan of Green's. In 2005, he asked Green to lend his rap skills to a song on the album *Twenty Six Inch*, which Danger Mouse was producing for New York rapper Jemini the Gifted One. After the session, Green was so impressed with what he'd heard he asked to record a couple of tracks with Danger Mouse.

But Danger Mouse didn't want to produce singles. He wanted to record an album with Green.

DANGER MOUSE

Danger Mouse was born Brian Burton on July 29, 1977, in White Plains, New York. His father was a teacher and his mother was a social worker. Burton and his family moved to an Atlanta suburb, where he was exposed to southern hip-hop music. At 18, he won a full scholarship to the University of Georgia, which introduced him to the music scene in Athens, Georgia. In 1995, Burton started deejaying in college while wearing a mouse costume to overcome his painful shyness and later switched to producing.

After changing his name to Danger Mouse, he became known for his "mash-ups"—mixtures of songs that didn't seem to go together but somehow harmonized perfectly. One of his most famous mash-ups blended rapper Jay-Z's *Black Album* with the British band the Beatles' famous *White Album*, which he called his *Grey Album*. Although it was never released, the album made the circuit of the local music scene and became well-known on the Internet. It helped Burton to land a job producing an album for the alternative British band Gorillaz.

The pair decided to form a musical duo, but were stumped on one thing—what to call themselves. They didn't want to be referred to as just "Cee Lo and Danger Mouse." So one night, Danger Mouse started discussing ideas for a name while having dinner with some friends. The result was a rather unusual name: Gnarls Barkley.

Green and Danger Mouse immediately connected through their music. "Gnarls Barkley was made out of me wanting to impress him, because I was so impressed by the music," Green said.[1]

‖‖‖

ST. ELSEWHERE

Gnarls Barkley recorded their groundbreaking 2006 collaboration, *St. Elsewhere,* with Green songwriting and singing and Danger Mouse producing. They paid for the production themselves, without support from a record company. As a result, they had total artistic freedom. "We just did whatever we wanted to do, and over time it turned into something that sounded thematic and natural," Danger Mouse said.[2]

CHARLES, OR GNARLS?

Although the name Gnarls Barkley sounds suspiciously similar to that of former National Basketball Association (NBA) player Charles Barkley, Danger Mouse insists it's just a coincidence. Danger Mouse has said he just liked the name and went with it, and there are no hidden meanings. In fact, the duo felt their chances of getting a record deal and releasing an album were so slim, they almost named their first album, *Danger Mouse and Cee-Lo: Who Cares?*

The freedom of recording their own music allowed Gnarls Barkley to pull inspiration from diverse influences. These included 1980s alternative music—such as a cover of the 1983 Violent Femmes song "Gone Daddy Gone"—as well as 1960s psychedelic music.

Instead of trying to get picked up by a major record company, Gnarls Barkley entrusted their first album to a start-up. The duo signed with Downtown Records in 2005, before the company had even launched. Downtown Records co-owner Josh Deutsch said, "We hadn't opened our office yet, but I convinced them that this would be the right home for them. It was a leap of faith on both sides."[3]

The album's title track, "St. Elsewhere," reflects Green's personal and professional struggles. In the song, Green sings, "I packed a few of my belongings / Left the life that I was living / Just some memories of it / Mostly the ones I can't forget."[4]

||||||||||||||||||||||||||||||||||||||||||||||||||||||||||

"CRAZY"

One of the tracks on *St. Elsewhere* is a quirky song called "Crazy." The song is about depression and mental illness and set to a catchy 1960s-influenced rhythm. No one expected that one song to turn Gnarls Barkley into a household name, but it did. "Crazy" reached the Top 5 on almost every record chart in Europe. *Rolling Stone* magazine named "Crazy" its Song of the Decade at the end of 2009. And the song helped Gnarls Barkley win the 2007 Grammy Award for Best Alternative Music Album, as well as an Album of the Year nomination.

Green was surprised by how fast the song caught on with listeners around the world. And he was blown away by the album's huge success. "We knew there would be some real highs when we

Gnarls Barkley performed at the 2006 MTV Movie Awards dressed as
Star Wars characters.

made the record," Green said. "We just weren't sure
what the highs would be."[5]

Why did "Crazy" get so big so quickly? Green
had a few ideas. "There's a lot of humanity and a lot
of humility in the song," he said. "I think it helps
describe and makes sense of a living condition that
we are all subjected to from time to time."[6]

"CRAZY" GOES NUTS

When Gnarls Barkley first released "Crazy," it got a chilly reception. Urban radio stations wouldn't play it, and neither would alternative stations. Then, in the winter of 2006, the duo uploaded the song onto the Internet. The song exploded. "Crazy" flew to the top of the United Kingdom singles chart and stayed there for nine weeks. In the United States, "Crazy" was downloaded more than 1.2 million times—making it the first song ever to reach Number 1 by downloads only. It hit Number 2 on the *Billboard* singles chart and eventually went platinum.

"Crazy" has been covered by artists ranging from Nelly Furtado to the Raconteurs. The video for the song won MTV VMAs for Best Editing and Best Direction. Green has described "Crazy" as "a tremor," saying, "That's how big it was in my soul."[7]

DOWNSIDES TO FAME

Touring is an important part of being a successful musician, and throughout the summer of 2006, Gnarls Barkley was constantly on the go. Danger Mouse and Green performed in front of 100,000 people at Lollapalooza in Grant Park in Chicago, Illinois, and headlined at the Montreux Jazz Festival in Switzerland. But Green wasn't a big fan of life on the road and preferred creating music to traveling.

Green has been known to dress up as superheroes, a habit he picked up when he was young. He's admitted that when he was a child, he wore a Batman costume just about everywhere he went.

Green has also described himself in heroic terms, as if he were saving the masses with his music: "As long as there is any justice in the world, I will be there."[9]

For Green, another downside to life on the road was leaving his family behind. Green remembered his own rebellious youth, spent without his father's guidance. He said,

> I'm happy to be touring. But I'm also a little saddened that my son has to go without me for extended periods of time. I don't want that pain for him. I don't want that absence, wonder, and idle time to fester into something negative, rebellious, or disobedient.[8]

||||||||||||||||||||||||||||||||||||||||||||||||||||||

THE ODD COUPLE

Gnarls Barkley became more than a musical collaboration for Green. It was a friendship, or "my safe haven and my sanctuary to expose or share and bring closure to my own issues," he said.[10]

In 2008, the duo released its second album. The title of the album, *The Odd Couple*, perfectly described the duo. Green was short and squat, while Danger Mouse was tall and lanky.

Though it was scheduled for an April 8 release, the album was leaked onto the Internet weeks before, forcing the record company to rush it into stores. Possibly because of its quick push into stores, the album had disappointing sales compared to Gnarls Barkley's previous release. In its first week, it only inched up to Number 18 on the *Billboard* album chart.

It did receive critical acclaim, however. *The Odd Couple* earned three Grammy nominations. The video for "Who's Gonna Save My Soul" was nominated for three MTV VMAs, including Breakthrough Video. In the video, a man rips out his own heart when his girlfriend breaks up with him at a diner. The heart then grows a pair of lips and begins singing in Green's voice.

GNARLS BARKLEY'S FASHION STATEMENT

If Green was known for his unusual fashion choices before Gnarls Barkley, his pairing with Danger Mouse doubled his eccentricity. The duo became almost as well-known for their crazy getups as for their music. They appeared at various concerts and photo shoots dressed as a bride and groom, Darth Vader and a Storm Trooper from *Star Wars*, Superman and Clark Kent, and the Cowardly Lion and Tin Man from *The Wizard of Oz*. Josh Deutsch, co-owner of their label Downtown Records, said these crazy costumes were calculated attempts to get attention for their music: "In every aspect of the campaign, we tried to establish the band as something unique and mysterious."[11]

SITTING AT THE TOP

Green had already had hints of success with Goodie Mob and his two solo records. But with Gnarls Barkley, he had become a true star. With the success came money—lots of it—but Green tried not to let the fame or fortune change him. One of the most important purchases Green did make, however, was a ranch about an hour outside of Atlanta.

Even winning at the Grammys—the pinnacle of success for most musicians—didn't seem to

Green enjoyed creative freedom through his collaboration
with Danger Mouse.

interest Green very much. Fame, he said, was not
what compelled him to make music. Yet fame did
have its benefits. After recording two albums with
Gnarls Barkley, Green was successful enough to
venture out on his own again. The resulting album
would be a surprise to the music industry.

||||||||||

With *The Lady Killer*, Green kept surprising critics and fans with his music.

CHAPTER 7
The Lady Killer

||||||||||||||||||||||||||||||||||||||||||||||||||||||||||||||||||||||||||||||||||||||

Fueled by the success of Gnarls Barkley, Green decided to try his luck again as a solo artist. When he released his album *The Lady Killer* in November 2010, Green's aim was to become a megastar—and to keep surprising those who thought they knew what to expect from him.

"For too long I've been underground and underdog," he said. "With this album, I wanted to say, 'Let me assure you that you don't know me completely."[1] Green signed on with a new management agency, Primary Wave Music, which has been responsible for steering the careers of artists such as Soulja Boy and 50 Cent. *The Lady Killer* was so important to Green, he insisted on being involved in every aspect of production.

Straying away from his hip-hop and rap roots, Green opted to work on this album with pop producers such as Salaam Remi, who had previously collaborated with singers Ricky Martin, Mary J. Blige, and Amy Winehouse. But the album stays true to Green's musical style, incorporating many of his influences, from 1970s disco to 1980s rock and alternative. He said the classic soul sounds of singers Al Green and Barry White and the band Earth, Wind and Fire also inspired the album. The album contains a fusion of streetwise soul and rock-and-roll sounds.

QUALITY OVER MONEY

Green has long felt that recording albums should be about much more than just making money. To him, the quality of the music always comes first. Green has expressed his frustration with the recording industry, which he believes welcomes too many artists regardless of their talent or ability to write meaningful music. "Not everyone should be allowed," Green has said.[2]

The name of the album—*The Lady Killer*—came from both his love and talent for attracting women and his style of music. Green said the name sounded "edgy and elegant at the same time."[3] But since Green had been writing and recording nonstop for three years, deciding which

> **"When I open my mouth to sing, I simply cannot help myself."[4]**
>
> —*CEE LO GREEN*

songs to include on the album wasn't easy. He had almost 70 songs ready to go. Green knew he had to narrow it down to 14 for the album. One of those 14 songs was destined to make both Green and *The Lady Killer* famous—and infamous.

A SONG SHOCKS AND AWES LISTENERS

Of all the tracks on *The Lady Killer*, none grabbed more attention than the single "[Forget] You." Some of the attention had to do with the song's

Singer-songwriter Bruno Mars teamed up with Green to write the popular song "[Forget] You."

catchy and retro sound. But the majority stemmed from the song's title, which contained an expletive, or an obscene word.

Green wrote "[Forget] You" with singer-songwriter Bruno Mars and his production team. They started with the title, including the expletive. With Mars on the piano and Green singing, they went back and forth creating lyrics and jamming until they'd written the whole song—

which took about two hours. While "[Forget] You" may seem like it's about losing a girlfriend to a rich guy, Green said it was actually written about the record company he never seemed to be able to please. He said,

> It was about my relationship with my label at that moment. I'd been recording for three years and I had over 70 songs, and I was ready to be heard. But my label was just sitting on it, and it was very disheartening, not knowing if what I was doing was good enough.[5]

Despite the obscene title, the song manages to be upbeat and fun. "It's very disarming, and it actually sounds nothing like that title—it's got a very tongue-in-cheek quality," Green said.[6]

PARENTAL CONSENT ||||||||||||||||||||||||||||||||||||||||||||||||||||||

Green was already a father when he released his controversial song "[Forget] You," which would make many parents consider changing the radio station or covering their children's ears. Did Green let his own son, Kingston, listen to it? Yes, he said, telling one reporter: "They grow up fast these days, and I've heard so much worse that they're already exposed to . . . so I figured my one song could not do any more damage."[7]

The problem came when the label decided to release the single. The record company couldn't put out a song featuring a curse word—much less expect it to hit the charts. So Green released a cleaner version of the single, titled "[Forget] You." An alternate version of the music video was also filmed.

|||||||||||||||||||||||||||||||||||||||||||||||||||||||||

PARODIES |||||||||||||||||||||||||||||||||||||||||||||||||||||||||||||||||||||||

One of the biggest moments for "[Forget] You" came when Gwyneth Paltrow sang it on the hit Fox series *Glee*. Paltrow guest starred on the show as a substitute teacher trying to prove to the students that she was hip and up on today's music. The episode drew 11.6 million viewers. Paltrow's performance was so popular many viewers purchased her cover on iTunes, making it Number 1 in downloads. Green was blown away by the actress' singing ability, saying, "I was impressed. I had no idea she was a vocalist. I thought it was great."[8] Paltrow wasn't the only celebrity to cover "[Forget] You." Former *Star Trek* actor William Shatner performed a heavily censored version on the late night talk show *Lopez Tonight*. The song also spawned several fan parodies, including "Stalk You" inspired by the social networking site Facebook, and "Block You," inspired by the video-sharing site YouTube.

GRAMMY NODS

"[Forget] You" became an instant Internet sensation in 2010. Millions of people watched both the clean and dirty versions of the music video on YouTube. The song reached Number 1 on the charts and became one of the most popular songs of the year. Green knew it was a catchy song, but he was still surprised by its success. He never thought a song with that kind of title would do so well. "It was such an immediate, overwhelming response," he said. "It's phenomenal, it's humbling, and it's empowering all at the same time."[9]

At the 2011 Grammy Awards on February 13, 2011, "[Forget] You" was nominated for Record of the Year and Song of the Year. But it wasn't the only song on *The Lady Killer* to get attention. At the 2012 Grammys on February 12, 2012, another single from the album, "Fool for You," won Grammys for Best R&B Song and Best Traditional R&B Performance.

Green also made headlines for his live performances of "[Forget] You" at both the 2011 Grammy Awards in February and the *Billboard* Music Awards in May 2011. During the middle of his *Billboard* Music Awards performance in Las Vegas, Nevada, Green continued playing as his piano flipped upside down over the audience.

|||||||||||||||||||||||||||||||||||||||||||||||||||||||||

GIVING BACK

Green had achieved the type of fame that most musicians only dream of. Reaching the top hadn't been easy, but he'd finally made it. "It's taken me 18 years to become an overnight sensation," he joked.[10]

With his success, Green decided to find a way to give back. In May 2011, Green joined battery manufacturer Duracell's Power Those Who Protect Us program, a battery donation program helping US firehouses with out-of-pocket power expenses. In support of the program, Green recorded a special version of "[Forget] You." The song, named "Thank You" instead, pays tribute to firefighters. Green wanted to show his support for firefighters, particularly after volunteer firefighters had rescued his mother during her near-fatal car accident. She was also a volunteer firefighter.

Green's partnership with Duracell was a cause close to his heart.

By 2011, Green was a multiplatinum recording artist and Grammy winner, conquering the music industry he felt had been trying to hold him back for so many years. Next, it was time to take on television.

||||||||||

Green made the leap onto the small screen in 2011 as a judge on *The Voice*.

CHAPTER 8

The Voice

||||||||||||||||||||||||||||||||||||||||||||||||||||

I n 2011, Green decided to try something new. He accepted a spot as a judge on the new NBC reality singing competition *The Voice*. This wasn't the first television show Green had been offered. According to Green, former *American Idol* judge Simon Cowell had also promised him a position on the American talent show *The X Factor*. *The X Factor* is similar to another show Cowell helped make famous— *American Idol*. Contestants sing in front of a panel of judges in the hope of winning a multimillion-dollar recording contract.

Even though Green liked Cowell and appreciated the offer, he turned it down in favor of *The Voice*. "I didn't see what made it distinctive enough," he said of *The X Factor*. "It kind of seemed like shows like *Idol* had run their course."[1]

Green said he preferred *The Voice* because the judges on the show are more like coaches, building

PRIME TIME GREEN

The Voice wasn't Green's only television appearance. He proved that he also had comedic talents when he showed up in an NBC promo for the sitcom *Parks and Recreation*, attempting to retrieve his *Voice* rotating chair from the show's Parks Department Director, Ron Swanson.

Green also appeared as a musical guest on *Saturday Night Live* with Gwyneth Paltrow. In one skit, a group of record executives led by Paltrow poked fun at the four-letter word in Green's famous song "[Forget] You" that caused so much trouble with the Federal Communications Commission. Green has even had his own show. He hosts *Cee Lo Green: Talking to Strangers*, named after one of his songs, on FUSE TV. On the show, he interviews other musicians about their music and careers. Rapper Lupe Fiasco and singers Keri Hilson and Kelly Rowland have been among his guests.

singers up rather than criticizing them like the judges on *The X Factor* and similar shows. He said,

> There's so much positive energy about this show and I'm not about . . . crushing peoples' dreams or judging people. I'm all about helping them, literally, which is the nature of this show and empowerment.[2]

The snub started a battle of words between the two men, with Cowell denying ever asking Green to be on *The X Factor*. Cowell also slammed *The Voice*, calling it nothing more than a rip-off of *The X Factor*. Meanwhile Green stood firmly behind his own show, saying if the two shows were in a ratings competition, *The Voice* would win.

|||||||||||||||||||||||||||||||||||||||||||||||||||||||||

THE VOICE

Appearing as a coach on *The Voice*, Green joined pop star Christina Aguilera, country singer Blake Shelton, and Maroon 5 lead singer Adam Levine. *The Voice* premiered on April 26, 2011, hosted by television personality Carson Daly.

The US version of *The Voice* is based on the show *The Voice of Holland,* a singing

PURRFECT THE CAT

Regular viewers of *The Voice* have probably noticed Green isn't alone while judging the show. He's often seen petting a fluffy white Persian cat. Green rescued the cat, named Purrfect, in 2012. Since then, they've formed a close bond. Purrfect even has her own page on the social networking site Twitter, where, not surprisingly, she regularly tweets about *The Voice*. She has more than 63,000 Twitter followers as of July 2012, as well as more than 22,000 "likes" on Facebook. After her debut on *The Voice*, Purrfect posted a message on her Facebook page that read, "Camera adds 10 lbs of fur, but I look purrrfect. Don't you agree?"[3] The spoiled feline also reportedly has an entourage of two trainers.

Purrfect was also part of a remix of the classic Meow Mix cat food jingle. As part of the promotion, for every download of the song, one pound (0.5 kg) of Meow Mix cat food was donated to the Pets Are Wonderful Support (PAWS) charity.

competition that first aired in the Netherlands in September 2010. Unlike other talent shows, *The Voice* is unique in that the four coaches sit in chairs that face *away* from the singers while they are performing. Only when a judge decides he or she likes the sound of a contestant's voice does he or she spin around to offer that person a spot on the show. Green liked the idea of judging based on talent instead of looks, saying,

While contestants audition, *The Voice* judges sit facing away from them.

It does encourage and embrace the underdog, as opposed to being cut down if you don't look a certain way. Because I don't look a certain way.[4]

Following the blind auditions, Green and the other coaches are each left with a team of singers who they mentor throughout the competition part of the show. During the battle rounds, two singers from the same team try to outperform each other, with their team coach making the final decision on who stays. Singers who survive the battle rounds move on to the live show performances. Viewers vote to choose a member from each team to send

With such popular singers sitting side-by-side as judges on *The Voice*, it made sense they eventually decided to collaborate musically. Aguilera sang on Maroon 5's 2011 hit "Moves Like Jagger," and in 2012, Green and Aguilera announced they were recording a song together for Aguilera's new album. Green also provided Shelton with a song originally intended to be a duet.

There has also been talk of a possible supergroup featuring all four singers. The four have already performed together once, covering Gnarls Barkley's hit "Crazy" on *The Voice* stage. Green said he liked the idea of doing an album with his fellow judges: "Why not, man? Why not? Everybody's talented. I think everybody would be up for it, man, because it's a great idea."[5]

home and the coaches then decide whether or not to save them. This leads to the final battle among the top four performers. One singer is ultimately crowned the winner.

||||||||||||||||||||||||||||||||||||||||||||||||||||||||||

COACH GREEN

The goal of Green and the other coaches is for one of their team members to become the show's winner. The winners of the show's first two seasons were Javier Colon from Levine's team and Jermaine

Paul from Shelton's team. Green's team members ended up finishing as runners-up in both seasons.

Mentoring young talent had proven to be an emotional experience for Green, who usually comes off as a tough guy. He became very attached to the talent on his teams, and even cried a few times on the show. On the March 26, 2012, episode of the second season, Green famously broke down when contestants Justin Hopkins and Tony Vincent sang the classic rock band Journey's song "Faithfully." At the end of the performance he told them, "I'm just in awe of you."[6] Vincent was equally in awe of his mentor. "Bringing tears to Cee Lo's eyes [is] incredibly humbling," he said.[7]

Green shed tears again when contestants James Massone and Wade sang Cyndi Lauper's song "True Colors." "This song moves people, that's what this song is doing right here," Green said.[8] Then he told

"I am here to serve the greater good, not only for myself but for my fellow man through the joy of music."[9]

—CEE LO GREEN

Left to right: The personalities of *The Voice* judges Shelton, Levine, Aguilera, Green, and host Daly have helped make the show an NBC hit.

the men, "That song made me cry, man. I'm proud of you all, man."[10]

The Voice was such a huge success during its first two seasons that a third season debuted in September 2012. All four of the judges returned for the third season. Green was reportedly paid $6 million to appear on the show, having promised to stay on *The Voice* at least until it got old. There was even talk in 2012 of Green replacing rapper will.i.am as a coach on the British version of *The Voice*.

||||||||||

Green has begun expanding his interests into writing and acting.

CHAPTER 9

Vegas and Beyond

||||||||||||||||||||||||||||||||||||||||||||

By 2012, Green was a Grammy-Award-winning musician and one of the hosts of a popular television singing competition. He'd performed just about every style of music in existence, including rap, hip-hop, pop, alternative, and rock. He'd been part of a band and a duo and had his own solo career. There was very little Green hadn't done . . . except possibly his own Las Vegas act.

During the 1950s and 1960s, famous performers made pilgrimages to perform in Las Vegas, a gambling mecca in the Nevada desert. For many in the entertainment industry, you weren't anybody until you saw your name in lights high above the Vegas strip. Iconic singers such as Sammy Davis Jr., Elvis Presley, and Frank Sinatra had all headlined shows in Vegas—so why not Green?

The pageantry of Las Vegas fit perfectly with Green's outrageous persona. "To do something young, fresh, and innovative, going to Vegas just seemed ideal," Green said.[1] Green was set to debut his own Vegas show in fall 2012, however in July 2012 it was postponed until spring 2013 to

LIBERACE

Green named his Las Vegas show, *Loberace*, after one of the most famous people ever to perform in that city: Liberace. A classically trained pianist, Liberace began entertaining in clubs during the early 1940s. In 1955, he opened a show at the Las Vegas Riviera Hotel. At the time, he was the highest-paid entertainer in Vegas. His shows became a regular attraction for visitors to the Las Vegas strip—and his name become synonymous with Las Vegas itself. Liberace continued to perform until his death in 1987 at the age of 67.

accommodate his *The Voice* filming schedule. Green named it *Loberace*, a tribute to the famous pianist Liberace.

The idea for Green's Vegas show came from his manager, Michael "Blue" Williams. Set to be performed in the Planet Hollywood Resort and Casino's 1,400-seat showroom, *Loberace* will be a journey through time—a magical, musical tribute to legends such as Prince and the Rolling Stones. It features special effects, magic, showgirls, and fantastic costumes. "The production will combine Cee Lo's flamboyant sense of style and over-the-top creativity," the show's producers said. "*Loberace* will be as inspired and visually alive as Cee Lo Green."[2]

Green was excited about the idea of performing in a city where so many other talented musicians had made their mark. He said:

> *I love the city. I can't wait to be a part of it. From this generation I would just like to be able to carry on, and pick up the torch, and continue to make Vegas a place to be.*[3]

Green has never been one to follow the beaten path—which hasn't always made him popular. During a performance on New Year's Eve 2011, Green ignited controversy by changing the lyrics to former Beatle member John Lennon's classic song "Imagine." He introduced the new lyrics while performing the song in Times Square on *New Year's Eve with Carson Daly*. Instead of singing the line "Nothing to kill or die for / and no religion too," he sang, "Nothing to kill or die for / and all religion's true."

Outrage came from both sides of the religious fence. Both evangelical Christians and atheists were furious at his suggestion that every religion was true. Lennon fans were also upset that Green would dare to change the lyrics of such a famous and beloved song. After receiving several angry tweets on Twitter, Green issued an apology. He wrote, "Yo I meant no disrespect by changing the lyric guys! I was trying to say a world where u could believe what you wanted that's all."[4]

GREEN SPARKLES ON SCREEN

Another medium Green still hadn't attempted was film. That changed in August 2012, when he made his acting debut in a remake of the 1976 movie *Sparkle*. The movie starred *American Idol* winner Jordin Sparks, who played an aspiring singer trying to make it in a Motown girl group similar to the Supremes.

Singer and actor Whitney Houston costarred in the film as Sparks's mother. It was supposed to have been Houston's comeback role. Sadly, in February 2012, six months before the film's release, Houston died in Beverly Hills, California. Green mourned the loss of his new friend. When he heard the news of her death, Green wrote on his Twitter account, "R.I.P. Sister WHITNEY HOUSTON!!!!!! We will always love you."[5]

More film roles were in Green's future. He provided the voice of Murray the Mummy in the

FUND-RAISER CONTROVERSY

Green made headlines again in March 2012 by singing an unedited version of "[Forget] You" at a fund-raiser for President Barack Obama. Green unleashed the profane song to an audience at Tyler Perry Studios in Atlanta. Green sang the song, complete with its off-color chorus. Obama didn't appear to get upset.

White House Press Secretary Jay Carney said Obama was actually a big Green fan—he reportedly had some of the singer's music on his iPod. Green fired back on Twitter in response to people upset over the incident. "All of you heard the song a thousand times so don't get all saint on me," he wrote.[6]

Green performed at the Super Bowl halftime show in 2012.

animated movie *Hotel Transylvania* and was mulling the possibility of future roles. He even said he'd consider becoming an actor full-time.

MEMOIRS

What could someone with as much experience in the entertainment industry as Green have to offer? Sharing those experiences in his memoirs, of course. Scheduled for publication in 2013 by Grand Central Publishing, Green's autobiography was still untitled as of August 2012. Green's coauthor was David Wild, a *Rolling Stone* magazine contributing editor. The book would chronicle Green's journey from Goodie Mob to world-renowned musician and star of *The Voice*. "You will enter into the supernatural, the surreal, the extraordinary. As Cee Lo Green, a.k.a. 'everybody's brother,' I will make you a believer," Green said of his memoirs.[7]

Grand Central Publishing said it was excited about the prospect of releasing Green's memoirs. Vice president and editor-in-chief of paperbacks Beth de Guzman said,

He dresses in sequined capes, performs with the Muppets and Madonna, and does 360-degree flips with a grand piano at his fingertips. Imagine all that outrageously unique and creative talent channeled into a book.[8]

GREEN FUTURE

Albums, television shows, movies, and more—Green has done it all, far exceeding his wildest dreams of fame. As of December 2011, Green earned a reported $20 million per year. He fronted one of the top reality entertainment shows on television. He had achieved a successful solo music career—as well as ongoing collaborations with former groups Goodie Mob and Gnarls Barkley.

In February 2012, Green announced he was working on his next solo album, *Cee-Lo Green . . . Is Everybody's Brother*, as well as a new album with Goodie Mob.

MOST CREATIVE

In 2012, Green added another honor to his résumé when *Fast Company* magazine ranked him number five on its list of the 100 Most Creative People in Business. Green appeared on the cover with his cat Purrfect. The magazine recognized Green for his long list of hyphenated titles, including "singer-writer-producer-personality-actor-entrepreneur-mentor-freak."[9] When *Fast Company* asked Green to describe himself, he replied, "I am a licensed, professional lady-killer."[10] The "lady" to whom he was referring wasn't a woman, however: it was the music industry.

Green hopes to continue inspiring and surprising fans with his music.

"I am music. It is my chemical makeup," Green has said.[11] Being at the top of his game allows Green to make such grand, often egotistical statements—and get away with them. "I don't have to do the music because my life depends on it," Green said. "I want to be able to do the music because life depends on it. You feel me?"[12] Apparently, millions of people around the world do.

TIMELINE

1974

Cee Lo Green is born Thomas DeCarlo Burton on May 30, in Atlanta, Georgia.

1976

Green's father dies of a heart attack.

1990

Green's mother, Sheila, is paralyzed in a near-fatal car accident.

1998

Goodie Mob releases its second album, *Still Standing*.

1999

Goodie Mob's third album, *World Party*, hits stores.

2000

Green marries Christina Shanta Johnson on March 18.

1992

Green's mother dies of injuries sustained in a car accident two years earlier.

1994

Green appears on OutKast's first album, *Southernplaya-listicadillacmuzik*.

1995

With the group Goodie Mob, Green releases his first album, *Soul Food*.

2000

Green's son, Kingston, is born.

2002

Green releases his first solo album, *Cee-Lo and His Perfect Imperfections*.

2004

Green's second album, *Cee-Lo Green . . . Is the Soul Machine*, is released.

TIMELINE

2004

Green writes the future Pussycat Dolls hit "Don't Cha."

2005

Green and Johnson divorce in August.

2006

With Danger Mouse, Green forms Gnarls Barkley and releases *St. Elsewhere.*

2010

As a solo artist, Green releases *The Lady Killer* in November; Gwyneth Paltrow sings "[Forget] You" on *Glee.*

2011

Green and Paltrow perform "[Forget] You" at the Grammy Awards on February 13.

2011

Green premieres as a judge on *The Voice* on April 26.

2007

Gnarls Barkley wins the 2007 Grammy for Best Alternative Music Album for *St. Elsewhere*.

2007

Green launches his own record label, Radiculture Records.

2008

Gnarls Barkley releases its second album, *The Odd Couple*.

2012

Green wins Grammys for Best R&B Song and Best Traditional R&B Performance on February 12.

2012

Green starts planning his 2013 Las Vegas show, *Loberace*.

2012

Green makes his film debut in the movie *Sparkle* in August.

FULL NAME

Thomas DeCarlo Callaway

DATE OF BIRTH

May 30, 1974

PLACE OF BIRTH

Atlanta, Georgia

MARRIAGE

Christina Johnson (2000–2005)

CHILDREN

Sierra, Kalah, and Kingston

SELECTED FILMS AND TELEVISION APPEARANCES

The Voice (2011–), *Sparkle* (2012), *Hotel Transylvania* (2012)

SELECTED ALBUMS

Cee-Lo Green and His Perfect Imperfections (2002), *Cee-Lo Green . . . Is the Soul Machine* (2004), *The Lady Killer* (2010), *Cee-Lo Green . . . Is Everybody's Brother* (2012)

SELECTED AWARDS

- Won 2007 Grammys for Best Alternative Music Album for Gnarls Barkley's *St. Elsewhere* (2006) and Best Urban/Alternative Performance for Gnarls Barkley's "Crazy"
- Won 2011 Grammy for Best Urban/Alternative Performance for "[Forget] You"
- Won 2012 Grammys for Best Traditional R&B Performance and Best R&B Song for "Fool for You"
- Nominated for 2011 Grammys for Record of the Year, Song of the Year, and Best Short Form Video for "[Forget] You"

PHILANTHROPY

Green partnered with Duracell's Power Those Who Protect Us program, a battery donation program to help US firehouses with out-of-pocket power expenses. Green remixed his song "[Forget] You" as "Thank You" as a tribute to firefighters.

"And success has been a long time coming, so to get so much love back is exhilarating. But I still feel like a normal person . . . I've walked the streets and I know what it feels like. I speak with humility, and apparently those songs connect with people."

—CEE LO GREEN

avant-garde—Something that is unusual or experimental.

conformist—A person who follows the same practices as most other people.

eloquent—Expressing oneself in a clear, intelligent way.

entourage—A group of attendants or associates of an important person.

falsetto—An artificially high singing voice.

flamboyant—Very unusual, elaborate, and flashy style that attracts attention.

genre—A category of art, music, or literature characterized by a particular style, form, or content.

Grammy Award—One of several awards the National Academy of Recording Arts and Sciences presents each year to honor musical achievement.

hip-hop—A style of popular music associated with US urban culture that features rap spoken against a background of electronic music or beats.

homage—Paying tribute to something or someone.

mainstream—The principal or dominant course, tendency, or trend.

memoir—A written account of one's experiences.

mentor—A trusted counselor or guide.

plumage—A bird's feathers.

psychedelic—Music inspired by the illegal drug culture of the 1960s.

synonymous—Something that has become interchangeable with another.

tongue-in-cheek—Not to be taken seriously or literally.

venue—A place where a concert or other event is held.

ADDITIONAL RESOURCES

SELECTED BIBLIOGRAPHY

"Cee-Lo Shares 'His Perfect Imperfections.'" *Billboard*. Billboard, 27 Apr. 2002. Web. 29 May 2012.

Frere-Jones, Sasha. "The Perfect Imperfections of Cee-Lo Green." *The Village Voice* 7 May 2002: 67–68. Print.

Linden, Amy. "The Fearless Cee Lo Green." *The Village Voice* 10 Nov. 2010: 52. Print.

Mulholland, Garry. "OMM: The first ten: 2: Down and Dirty: Cee Lo Green is the Soul Machine." *The Observer* 25 Apr. 2004: 44. Print.

FURTHER READINGS

Belmont & Belcourt Biographies. *Cee Lo Green: An Unauthorized Biography*. Chicago: Price World, 2012. Print.

Cornish, Melanie J. *The History of Hip-Hop*. New York: Crabtree, 2009. Print.

WEB SITES

To learn more about Cee Lo Green, visit ABDO Publishing Company online at **www.abdopublishing.com**. Web sites about Cee Lo Green are featured on our Book Links page. These links are routinely monitored and updated to provide the most current information available.

PLACES TO VISIT

The Grammy Museum

800 W. Olympic Boulevard, Los Angeles, CA 90015-1300
213-765-6800
www.grammymuseum.org
The Grammy Museum features exhibits related to many genres of music.

Las Vegas, Nevada

702-892-0711
www.visitlasvegas.com
Green was scheduled to launch his Las Vegas show, *Loberace*, in 2013.

SOURCE NOTES

CHAPTER 1. A NIGHT WITH THE MUPPETS

1. "Cee Lo Green Muppet Outfit Vs. Lady Gaga Egg Thing: Grammy Fight!" *CBS News.* CBS Interactive, 14 Feb. 2011. Web. 18 June 2012.

2. "'The Voice' Star Cee-Lo Green—WSJ Exclusive Interview." *YouTube.* YouTube, 3 Feb. 2012. Web. 26 Sept. 2012.

3. "The Year of Gnarls." *Chicago Tribune* 28 Dec. 2006: 42. Print.

4. Bridget Bland. "20 Questions With Grammy Award Winning, Alternative Hip Hop/Soul Crooner Cee Lo Green." *Entertainment Newswire.* Black Voices, 7 Feb. 2011. Web. 8 Aug. 2012.

CHAPTER 2. BECOMING CEE LO

1. John Dingwall. "Cee Lo Green: I May Swear in My New Song But I Minister to People Through Music." *Daily Record.* Daily Record, 8 Oct. 2010. Web. 28 Aug. 2012.

2. Cee Lo Green. "The Secrets of My Success." *Mail on Sunday* 3 July 2011: 32. Print.

3. Caspar Llewellyn Smith. "Q&A." *Guardian* 14 Nov. 2010: 5. Print.

4. John Dingwall. "Cee Lo Green: I May Swear in My New Song But I Minister to People Through Music." *Daily Record.* Daily Record, 8 Oct. 2010. Web. 28 Aug. 2012.

5. Peter Lauria. "Cee Lo Uncensored." *The Daily Beast.* CNN, 20 Jan. 2011. Web. 7 Aug. 2012.

6. Caspar Llewellyn Smith. "Q&A." *Guardian* 14 Nov. 2010: 5. Print.

7. "Cee Lo Distilled." *YouTube.* YouTube, 24 June 2011. Web. 8 Aug. 2012.

8. Ibid.

CHAPTER 3. GOODIE MOB

1. Mosi Reeves. "Crazy about Cee-Lo." *Creative Loafing Atlanta.* Creative Loafing Atlanta, 20 Sept. 2006. Web. 3 May 2012.

2. Shawnee Smith. "Goodie Mob. Stands On Its Message." *Billboard* 110.18 (1998): 25. *Academic Search Premier.* Web. 9 Aug. 2012.

3. Bret Love. "Son of a Preacher Man." *Georgia Music Magazine.* Georgia Music Magazine, Fall 2011. Web. 23 May 2012.

4. "She Knows Lyrics." *MetroLyrics.* CBS Interactive Music Group, n.d. Web. 8 Aug. 2012.

5. Bret Love. "Son of a Preacher Man." *Georgia Music Magazine.* Georgia Music Magazine, Fall 2011. Web. 23 May 2012.

6. Lisa Robinson. "Cee Lo Green." *Vanity Fair* 616 (2011): 100. *MasterFILE Premier.* Web. 8 Aug. 2012.

7. Maurice G. Garland. "A Dirty Job for Goodie Mob." *Creative Loafing Atlanta.* Creative Loafing Atlanta, 15 Sept. 2009. Web. 22 May 2012.

8. Bret Love. "Son of a Preacher Man." *Georgia Music Magazine.* Georgia Music Magazine, Fall 2011. Web. 23 May 2012.

9. Ibid.

10. Daniel Kreps. "Cee-Lo and Goodie Mob To Reunite For September Concert in Atlanta." *Rolling Stone.* Rolling Stone, 3 Aug. 2009. Web. 24 May 2012.

CHAPTER 4. CEE LO GOES SOLO

1. David Basham. "Goodie M.O.B.'s Cee-Lo To Tie The Knot." *MTV*. MTV, 14 Mar. 2000. Web. 24 May 2012.

2. Tom Horan. "Cee Lo Green: There's No One Doing Anything Quite Like I Do." *The Telegraph*. Telegraph Media Group, 2 Nov. 2010. Web. 18 June 2012.

3. David Basham. "Goodie M.O.B.'s Cee-Lo To Tie The Knot." *MTV*. MTV, 14 Mar. 2000. Web. 24 May 2012.

4. Craig Mclean. "Captain America: Why Everyone Wants to Be on Cee Lo Green's Team." *Independent*. Independent, 3 July 2011. Web. 24 May 2012.

5. "Sierra Symone: Not Your Average Daddy's Girl." *Thesavvygal.com*. Thesavvygal. com, 19 Sept. 2011. Web. 24 May 2012.

6. Caspar Llewellyn Smith. "Q&A." *Guardian* 14 Nov. 2010: 5. Print.

7. "Cee-Lo Shares 'His Perfect Imperfections." *Billboard*. Billboard, 27 Apr. 2002. Web. 29 May 2012.

8. Ibid.

9. Mosi Reeves. "Crazy about Cee-Lo." *Creative Loafing Atlanta*. Creative Loafing Atlanta, 20 Sept. 2006. Web. 8 Aug. 2012.

10. "Cee-Lo Shares 'His Perfect Imperfections." *Billboard*. Billboard, 27 Apr. 2002. Web. 29 May 2012.

11. Will Hermes. "Cee-Lo Green & His Perfect Imperfections." *Entertainment Weekly*. Entertainment Weekly, 26 Apr. 2002. Web. 29 May 2012.

12. Mosi Reeves. "Crazy about Cee-Lo." *Creative Loafing Atlanta*. Creative Loafing Atlanta, 20 Sept. 2006. Web. 8 Aug. 2012.

13. "'The Voice' Star Cee-Lo Green—WSJ Exclusive Interview." *YouTube*. YouTube, 3 Feb. 2012. Web. 26 Sept. 2012.

14. Mary Awosika. "Cee-Lo Green Ministers to the Faithful." *Sarasota Herald Tribune*, 22 Oct. 2004: 7. Print.

15. Ibid.

16. Garry Mulholland. "Cee-lo Green: Is the Soul Machine." *TheObserver*. Guardian.co.uk, 25 Apr. 2004. Web. 8 Aug. 2012.

CHAPTER 5. STRUGGLES

1. Mike Pattenden. "Elton John and Freddie Mercury Inspire Me, Says Gnarls Barkley's Cee Lo Green." *Mail Online*. Daily Mail, 2 July 2011. Web. 8 Aug. 2012.

2. Mosi Reeves. "Crazy about Cee-Lo." *Creative Loafing Atlanta*. Creative Loafing Atlanta, 20 Sept. 2006. Web. 8 Aug. 2012.

3. Iona Kirby. "Cee Lo Green Was Arrested in 2001 After Threatening Then-Wife Christina Johnson." *MailOnline*. Daily Mail, 2 May 2012. Web. 2 May 2012.

4. Mosi Reeves. "Crazy about Cee-Lo." *Creative Loafing Atlanta*. Creative Loafing Atlanta, 20 Sept. 2006. Web. 8 Aug. 2012.

5. Ibid.

6. "Cee Lo Green: Such A 'Lady Killer." *All Things Considered*. National Public Radio, 17 Nov. 2010. Radio.

7. Ibid.

8. Mosi Reeves. "Crazy about Cee-Lo." *Creative Loafing Atlanta*. Creative Loafing Atlanta, 20 Sept. 2006. Web. 8 Aug. 2012.

9. Jody Rosen. "Cee-Lo Green: The Lady Killer." *Rolling Stone*. Rolling Stone, 8 Nov. 2010. Web. 4 June 2012.

10. Caspar Llewellyn Smith. "Q&A." *Guardian* 14 Nov. 2010: 5. Print.

CHAPTER 6. GNARLS BARKLEY

1. Mosi Reeves. "Crazy about Cee-Lo." *Creative Loafing Atlanta*. Creative Loafing Atlanta, 20 Sept. 2006. Web. 8 Aug. 2012.

2. Ibid.

3. Ibid.

4. "St. Elsewhere Lyrics." *MetroLyrics*. CBS Interactive, n.d. Web. 23 Aug. 2012.

5. "The Year of Gnarls." *Chicago Tribune* 28 Dec. 2006: 42. Print.

6. Michael Endelman. "Gnarls in Charge." *Entertainment Weekly*. Entertainment Weekly, 7 Dec. 2006. Web. 31 May 2012.

7. Cian Traynor. "Interview: Cee-Lo Green." *Stool Pigeon*. Stool Pigeon, 8 Oct. 2010. Web. 8 Aug. 2012.

8. Mosi Reeves. "Crazy about Cee-Lo." *Creative Loafing Atlanta*. Creative Loafing Atlanta, 20 Sept. 2006. Web. 8 Aug. 2012.

9. John Dingwall. "Cee Lo Green: I May Swear in My New Song But I Minister to People Through Music." *Daily Record*. Daily Record, 8 Oct. 2010. Web. 28 Aug. 2012.

10. Jeff Chang. "First Came Crazy, Now Comes Odd." *New York Times*. New York Times, 6 Apr. 2008. Web. 23 May 2012.

11. Mosi Reeves. "Crazy about Cee-Lo." *Creative Loafing Atlanta*. Creative Loafing Atlanta, 20 Sept. 2006. Web. 8 Aug. 2012.

CHAPTER 7. *THE LADY KILLER*

1. Austin Scaggs. "Q&A: Cee Lo Green." *Rolling Stone* 9 Dec. 2010: 26. Print.

2. "'The Voice' Star Cee-Lo Green—WSJ Exclusive Interview." *YouTube*. YouTube, 3 Feb. 2012. Web. 26 Sept. 2012.

3. "Cee Lo Green: Such A 'Lady Killer.'" *All Things Considered*. National Public Radio. 17 Nov. 2010. Radio.

4. "On The Record: Cee Lo Green (January 2011)." *YouTube*. YouTube, 4 Jan. 2011. Web. 8 Aug. 2012.

5. Eric Spitznagel. "Cee Lo Green Is Fking Outrageous." *Esquire*. Hearst Communications, 5 Feb. 2012. Web. 4 June 2012.

6. Austin Scaggs. "Q&A: Cee Lo Green." *Rolling Stone* 9 Dec. 2010: 26. Print.

7. Caspar Llewellyn Smith. "Q&A." *Guardian* 14 Nov. 2010: 5. Print.

8. "'I'm a Granddad at 35,' Gnarls Barkley Star Cee Lo Green Celebrates Daughter's New Baby." *MailOnline*. Daily Mail, 3 Dec. 2010. Web. 2 May 2012.

9. "People: A Few Words with Cee Lo." *Dallas Morning News*. Dallas Morning News, 12 Dec. 2010. Web. 02 Aug. 2012.

10. Lisa Robinson. "Cee Lo Green." *Vanity Fair* 616 (2011): 100. *MasterFILE Premier*. Web. 8 Aug. 2012.

CHAPTER 8. *THE VOICE*

1. Jill Serjeant. "Cee Lo Green Crosses 'X' Off the List and Finds His '*Voice*.'" *Washington Post* 16 Apr. 2011: C.5. Print.

2. Erin Carlson. "'*Voice*' Judge Cee Lo Green Shrugs Off 'X Factor' Competition." *Hollywood Reporter.* Hollywood Reporter, 5 Apr. 2012. Web. 9 June 2012.

3. Iona Kirby. "Pawing His Way to the Top." *Mail Online.* Daily Mail, 15 Feb. 2012. Web. 9 June 2012.

4. Lisa Robinson. "Cee Lo Green." *Vanity Fair* 616 (2011): 100. *MasterFILE Premier*. Web. 8 Aug. 2012.

5. Associated Press. "Cee Lo Green Says He's Sticking With '*Voice*.'" *MySanAntonio. com.* San Antonio Express-News, 9 May 2012. Web. 10 June 2012.

6. Jennifer Kamm. "Cee Lo Green Cried 3 Times During 'The Voice'" *HollywoodLife.* PMC, 27 Mar. 2012. Web. 18 Apr. 2012.

7. Ibid.

8. Laura Schreffler. "Break Out the Tissues!" *Mail Online.* Daily Mail, 27 Mar. 2012. Web. 9 June 2012.

9. Associated Press. "Cee Lo Green says he's sticking with '*Voice*.'" *MySanAntonio. com.* San Antonio Express-News, 9 May 2012. Web. 10 June 2012.

10. Laura Schreffler. "Break Out the Tissues!" *Mail Online.* Daily Mail, 27 Mar. 2012. Web. 9 June 2012.

CHAPTER 9. VEGAS AND BEYOND

1. Whitney Pastorek. "Cee Lo Green: How to Ride Your Creativity." *Fast Company.* Fast Company, 14 May 2012. Web. 7 Aug. 2012.

2. Brennan Williams. "Cee Lo Green Announces Las Vegas Residency." *Huffington Post.* Huffington Post, 2 Mar. 2012. Web. 8 Aug. 2012.

3. Ibid.

4. Frank Lovece. "Cee Lo Drops Notes Apology Thread Erased After Changing Lennon Lyric." *Newsday* 4 Jan. 2012: A.14. Print.

5. CNN Wire Staff. "Stunned Celebrities Mourn Whitney Houston." *CNN Entertainment.* CNN, 12 Feb. 2012. Web. 17 June 2012.

6. Jennifer Brett. "Cee-Lo Flips Bird, Drops F-Bomb at Obama Fundraiser." *The Buzz.* AJC.com, 19 Mar. 2012. Web. 18 Apr. 2012.

7. "Cee Lo Green Is Writing His Memoirs." *Billboard.* Billboard, 28 Feb. 2012. Web. 4 May 2012.

8. Ibid.

9. Whitney Pastorek. "Cee Lo Green: How to Ride Your Creativity." *Fast Company.* Fast Company, 14 May 2012. Web. 7 Aug. 2012.

10. Ibid.

11. Ibid.

12. Ibid.

ABOUT THE AUTHOR

Stephanie Watson is a freelance writer based in Atlanta, Georgia. Over her 20-plus-year career, she has written for television, radio, the Web, and print. Watson has authored more than two dozen books, including, *Celebrity Biographies: Daniel Radcliffe*, *Heath Ledger: Talented Actor*, and *Anderson Cooper: Profile of a TV Journalist*.

PHOTO CREDITS